Everything You Need to Know

WHEN YOU ARE THE VICTIM OF A VIOLENT CRIME

In many neighborhoods people live behind fences and bars to protect themselves and their possessions.

• THE NEED TO KNOW LIBRARY •

Everything You Need to Know

WHEN YOU ARE THE VICTIM OF A VIOLENT CRIME

Jed Palmer

THE ROSEN PUBLISHING GROUP, INC.
NEW YORK

Published in 1994, 1998 by The Rosen Publishing Group, Inc.
29 East 21st Street, New York, New York, 10010

Revised Edition 1998

Library of Congress Cataloging-in-Publication Data

Palmer, Jed.
    Everything you need to know when you're the victim of a violent
crime / Jed Palmer.
      p.   cm.
    Includes bibliographical references and index.
    ISBN 0-8239-2622-2 (lib. binding)
    1. Victims of crimes—United States—Juvenile literature. 2. Victims of
crimes—United States—Psychology—Juvenile literature. 3. Victims of
crimes—Legal status, laws, etc.—United States—Juvenile literature. 4.
Crime prevention—United States—Juvenile literature. [1. Victims of
crime. 2. Crime prevention.] I. Title.
    HV6250.3U5P35 1994
    362.88'0973—dc20   94-6042
                                                  CIP
                                                  AC

Manufactured in the United States of America

Contents

Introduction

Nobody expects to be a victim of violent crime. If you or someone you know has been victimized by violent crime, then you understand how shocking and upsetting violence can be. After the crime you begin to question everyone and everything. But you find no answers. Violent crime doesn't ever make sense. It almost always comes without reason and can happen to anyone at any time. Often it is just bad luck—being in the wrong place at the wrong time. There is nothing the victim or anyone else can do to avoid the situation.

This lack of control is one of the most difficult parts of a crime for the victim to accept. Victims of violence often try to figure out why they were chosen as the victim, why they were targeted. Some wonder if they did something wrong, or if they somehow deserved their pain. Others bury the memories and try to forget about the incident. Many victims become depressed or angry. Each of these reactions, though painful, is normal. The most important thing to remember is that you survived the attack and that you will be okay.

This book will help you learn and understand the necessary tools to cope with a violent attack. It explains what violent crime is and talks about the different kinds of emotions that victims experience. This book encourages you to get help for your anger, depression, and denial. It educates you on the process involved in bringing your attacker to justice. It provides practical steps you can take to make yourself safer from violent criminals.

Emotional and physical recovery from a violent crime can be a long process. The victim will need to talk with friends, family, and sometimes a professional counselor about the way he or she is feeling. The family and friends of the victim may be unsure of how to act around the victim. There is often police involvement and perhaps a trial following a violent attack. This book will explain how the law works for you when you are a victim.

Continuing your life after a violent crime is difficult. This book will help you learn to successfully cope with your anger and fear and possibly help you bring your assailant to justice.

More and more school systems are asking police officers to visit the classrooms and speak to the students about becoming "street-smart."

Chapter 1

The Problem of Violent Crime

We hear about violent crime every day. It is on the evening news, in the newspapers, and dramatized on shows we watch on television. All neighborhoods in every part of the country are affected by violence.

The threat of violence is always around even if you never see guns, drugs, or gangs. This is a scary thought and can create a fear that affects the decisions you make every day. The thought of being confronted violently can change the way you look at yourself and at those around you. You may be afraid of going to certain sections of town or you may want to avoid going out alone. If you've ever been threatened by a stranger, the threat of violence may make you less willing to talk to any person who is different than you—different gender, skin color, age group, or social group. In this way, the fear of violence can dictate where you go, when you go, and with whom you talk.

No One Is Immune

If you or someone you know has been victimized
by a violent crime, you understand that no one is
immune to it. You may feel afraid a lot. This is normal.
For many victims, the psychological damage caused
by a violent attack can be much more painful than a
physical injury. It may be hard for a victim or the
friend of a victim to understand how other people can
seem carefree about violence. Many adults may seem
to be completely unafraid of going places or talking
to people who may scare you. Because you or someone
you know has been victimized, you are immediately
aware of the fact that a violent crime can be committed by anyone at any time. Other people are aware of
this, but if they have not seen it first hand, then they
can dismiss their fears easier than you can.

Defining the Problem

The best way to cope with violent crime is to understand exactly what it is and how it usually occurs.
The Federal Bureau of Investigation (FBI) defines violent crime as any of five different offenses: homicide
(murder), rape, robbery, sexual assault, and aggravat-
ed assault (hitting someone with the intent to cause
harm). These are the technical names for a more basic
idea. A violent crime is any unlawful act that uses or
even threatens to use physical force.

Violence often stems from anger; in many cases anger
at someone or something completely unrelated to the victim. It sometimes comes from jealousy, perhaps over a

Constant fear and depression may be reactions to having
been a victim of a violent crime.

girlfriend or boyfriend. Sometimes the attacker is delu-
sional or paranoid from drug use. Whatever reasons
the attacker may claim, there is no acceptable excuse.
Violent crime is always wrong and never makes sense.

Each year, the United States Department of Justice
interviews victims of violent crime to determine how
many of these crimes occurred in the past year. The
following statistics, taken from the 1995 Department
of Justice report, show how common violent crime is
in the United States.

- There were close to 1.8 million violent offenses in 1995.
- For every 1,000 people aged two or older, there occurred two rapes or attempted rapes, two assaults with serious injury, and five robberies.
- Young people, African-Americans, and males were most vulnerable to violent crime.
- One in nine people ages twelve to fifteen were victims of violent crime. One in 196 people age sixty-five or more were victimized.
- Violence affected one in sixteen African-Americans, compared to one in twenty Caucasians.
- One in twenty-four females and one in seventeen males suffered from violent crime in 1995.
- Over 106,000 episodes of violent crime occurred in suburban areas, and almost 75,000 incidents took place in rural areas.

With so many crimes occurring each year, it may seem difficult for anybody to claim that violent crime cannot find them. Still, this is what most people do. Until it happens to you, or to someone close to you, it seems easy to ignore the problem.

Unfortunately, violent crime is real. It knows no limit. Black or white, female or male, rich or poor, young or old, you are a potential victim. Pretending that the problem doesn't exist will not make you any safer. If you have been the victim of or a witness to a violent crime, then you know that no matter where you live or who you are, crime can find you. Your best defense is to accept the prevalence of crime in our society and to educate yourself about how to minimize the chance of you becoming a victim of violent crime.

Violence at School

Schools, playgrounds, quiet streets, and parking lots are the scenes of muggings, assaults, and kidnappings every day. Much depends on where you live and go to school, but even the safest neighborhoods can be the target of serious crime.

After school every day, Steven walked to the high school to ride home with his big brother. Part of his route included a path that went through the woods. Steven never worried about taking this path because his town was quiet and safe.

After an evening band practice, Steven left his school to go meet his brother. It was 6:00 p.m and getting dark when Steven turned onto the path. He could see other people ahead of him on the path and could hear kids playing close by.

Halfway down the path, Steven saw a high school boy bent over, as if tying his shoe. Steven didn't know him. As Steven came closer, the boy stood up and walked towards Steven. At first, Steven thought that maybe he needed directions. Instead, he stood in Steven's path and demanded money. Steven thought it was a high-school joke. His brother's friends often acted serious when they were just kidding. Steven tried

Portable metal-scanning devices are used in some school systems to search for weapons.

to walk past him. With no warning, the boy pushed Steven to the ground.

The boy reached into his jacket and pulled out a knife. He demanded Steven's money again. Steven was so surprised he didn't know what to do. All he could see was the knife. He dropped his money onto the ground and backed up. He ran all the way back to the junior high school where he told his band teacher what happened. The teacher listened to his story and drove him to the high school.

As many as 22 percent of all students, boys and girls, in the United States report being the victim of a violent crime in school. Many more crimes go unreported because the victims are afraid of being attacked again by the same person or group.

Parents of schoolchildren are often horrified to hear stories about the violence in schools. Thirty years ago kids also got into fights, but almost always with their fists. Knives were rare, and guns were almost unheard of. The deadly fights that happen in today's schools are a big problem. In one national study, as many as 4 percent of students grades nine through twelve reported having taken a gun to school. Over twice as many admit to bringing knives, razor blades, chains, brass knuckles, and other small weapons. Some of these kids are members of gangs, some are not. Many of them bring weapons to school in order to protect themselves from other kids with weapons.

Rebecca didn't want to go to school. Three other girls had formed a gang. One of these three girls accused Rebecca of trying to steal her boyfriend, and now all three girls hated Rebecca. Last week, one of them pushed her down in the hallway. Yesterday, one of the girls spat at her and told her that her gang was going to beat her up.

Rebecca's mother refused to let her skip school. On her way to the school bus, Rebecca stopped in the garage and took a box-cutter from her dad's tool box. She had never used a knife before and didn't think she would be very good in a fight. Still, she hoped to use it to scare the other girls away.

As the statistics and stories show, you can be a victim when you least expect it. In Steven's case, the crime was sudden and he was totally unprepared. There was little he could do to protect himself. For Rebecca, school had become a place of fear, although she knew she had to go to class anyway. Both of these teens suffered the threat of violent crime. Whether you have been made a victim or not, the first step to coping with violent crime is understanding that violent crime is not a punishment for being silly or foolish. Violent crime is always wrong, and never the fault of the victim.

Chapter 2

What to Do If It Happens to You

No one can guarantee your safety anywhere. But with some preparation you can help to make a dangerous situation safer. You can increase your control over what happens to you.

Be Prepared

If you've ever been to school, you know what a fire drill is. You may think of it only as something that takes you out of class for five minutes, but the purpose of a fire drill is knowledge. If there ever is a fire in your school, you'll know what to do because you've been lining up and walking out for years.

Violent crime deserves the same sort of preparation. You can't always prevent a violent crime from occurring. But just as you can learn how to survive a fire by keeping calm, you can train yourself to survive a violent attack. The best thing is to try to avoid circumstances where a violent attack may be more likely to occur. But this cannot always be done.

Let's say that you are walking down a dark street. It's late and you are feeling nervous. You hear footsteps behind you. They sound like they are getting faster. What do you do?

Trust your instincts. If something feels wrong, it probably is. Don't take any chances. Cross the street and walk toward an open store, restaurant, or lighted house. Find a safe place as quickly as possible. Once you are safe, tell someone you trust about your experience.

Keep moving. You're an easier target if you are standing still, so keep moving toward a destination. If anyone wants to cause trouble, they'll have to catch up, and you'll have a few extra moments to run or call for help. If someone yells to you asking directions or for help with something be careful. Most people are perfectly safe, but there's no way to know. When you're alone, always play it safe.

Make some noise. Attract attention if you're in trouble. Yell and scream as loud as you can. Protect yourself by alerting the people around you.

Pay attention. Know where you are and what is happening. Noticing whether other people or buildings are near or far might help you decide what to do next.

Be aware of your attacker and your surroundings. Once the attacker is gone, you will want to give the police as much description as possible about the attacker's face, body, clothing, and voice. The more the police know, the better the chances are that they will

An intercom system allows you to identify a visitor before you open your door.

catch your attacker.

It's just money. Try to end an attack as quickly as possible by surrendering your valuables without a fight. They can be replaced, but your life cannot. Always put your safety first.

Know where to go. Report any crime to the police immediately even if you know the attacker personally. The quicker they are informed, the more likely it is that your attacker will be picked up. If you need medical help, get to a hospital as soon as possible.

Sit down with you parents or a teacher to discuss the safest routes to take home from school, the gym, work, the library, and wherever else you spend time. Designate stores and friends' houses to be your "safe places." Whenever you feel threatened you can go to your nearest safe place and get help.

•Always tell your parents and friends where you'll be and how long you'll be there. If you change plans, let someone know where you are.

•Make a safety plan for home, too. Discuss the plan with your parents. For example:

•Never open the door before you know who is on the other side.

•Do not tell a stranger on the phone or behind the door that you are home alone. If he or she is asking for your parent say that your mom or dad is occupied at the moment, and take a message or tell the person to come back at a time when your parent will be home.

•Be careful of delivery persons. If you get nervous

A good way to stay safe—wherever you are—is to always be aware of what is going on around you.

when someone is at the door, ask them to just leave the package. Don't be afraid or embarrassed to be safe.

•Plan an escape route from your house. If you feel threatened by someone outside the door, use this route to leave and go to the safe place nearest you. Call your parents or the police for help.

Staying Calm and "The Freeze"

Constantly worrying about being the victim of violent crime won't do you any good. Not only will you make yourself "crazy," but you will become an easy target for criminals. Being in control of yourself and looking confident is the safest way to walk down any street.

It is important to remain as calm as possible during the crime as well. This can be the hardest time to control yourself. It's very difficult to do anything but be scared when someone is threatening you. But the best way to keep yourself safe is not to panic. You will help yourself the most by thinking clearly.

When you feel threatened, your body tries to help you deal with the situation. It produces adrenaline, which is a stimulant that is helpful under stress. It can make you much quicker and stronger than usual. There are many amazing stories of people showing superhuman strength and quickness during life-threatening situations because of adrenaline—like a mother who lifted the rear end of a car single-handedly to free her child pinned under the wheel. Too much adrenaline, however, can make your body freeze up. Some people have trouble doing anything at all when they are very frightened.

Sarah lives in the city. The walk home after school was always better when Sarah took her special shortcut. As she walked through an empty alley, two young men stepped out of the shadows and pushed Sarah against a wall. One asked for money as he held a brick over her head. The other gripped Sarah's arm and stroked her face. She was terrifed. She tried to tell him about the money in her sock. She even tried to point to it. But she could not force herself to move. She was paralyzed. She felt like she was screaming inside, but she couldn't make a sound. Her eyes were locked open. Her body felt absolutely stiff.

It is common for victims to freeze up like this at the time of an attack. Many victims feel badly about freezing because they feel helpless and under someone else's control. If you have experienced this do not be angry with yourself or feel ashamed. Your stillness may have kept the criminal from feeling threatened, which often prevents the violence from escalating. Sometimes it allows the crime be over with quickly and without any bloodshed.

Try to imagine what an attack might feel like. Imagine yourself staying calm and doing whatever the attacker asks in order to remain safe. Speak with an expert such as a policeman or a self-defense instructor about what happens during an attack. Taking a self-defense course at your school or at a local gym my be a good idea. You can never be sure how you'll react under stress, but knowledge may give you the confidence to stay cool and to protect yourself during an attack.

Many young women are becoming knowledgeable in the use of firearms.

Defending Yourself and Running Away

Different people react in different ways when they are the victims of violent crime. Some react with shock, unable to do anything. Others react with anger. Sometimes the victim is so surprised by the attack that he or she strikes back instantly against the attacker. This is an automatic reaction without planning or thought. It can be very dangerous to respond to a criminal in this way.

Many people feel threatened enough to buy tools for self-defense. Some carry aerosol containers of chemicals that can disable an attacker when sprayed into the face. Others carry whistles and "screamers." If they feel threatened or under attack, they pull the screamer out and turn it on. It makes an extremely loud noise, which can frighten the attacker and draw the attention of others.

Many ordinary people learn to protect themselves by taking special classes in the martial arts, such as karate or kung fu. Others feel so threatened by violent crime that they carry weapons, such as knives and guns. They want to have equal force against any attacker. But many people argue that carrying a knife or gun only results in a more dangerous society. Most people do agree that training and experience are required when dealing with any sort of weapon, especially a gun. All things considered, the best choice may be to leave "policework" to the police. In most situations, taking aggressive action against a criminal is a bad idea. It is likely that you will get yourself into more trouble if you challenge or pursue an attacker.

Sometimes, however, defending yourself is your only choice. If you feel sure that your attacker means to hurt you, fight back with all your strength any way that you can. The best places to attack are the eyes, the throat, the groin, and the shin and knee areas. If you are close, strike with your knees and elbows. Don't be afraid to hurt your attacker. When you decide you must fight back, don't go halfway. But never forget where you are and what is happening. When you see your chance to run, take it. Remember: you do not want to be there.

Any time you are under attack, the best choice is always running away. Some people consider running away a shameful or cowardly thing to do. If you believe that, you put yourself in danger every time you leave the house. The best proof of bravery and intelligence is your own survival. And the best way to survive is by paying attention and looking for a way to escape. Make sure you get to a safe place, and then get to a phone. Call the police immediately.

It is important to remember that there is no definite right or wrong way to react to a rape, mugging, or any other violent attack. Every situation is different. Every person is different. Be informed and aware. Figure out your choices and don't be afraid to act.

Chapter 3

Recovering from a Violent Crime

Victims of violent crime often find getting back to "normal" very difficult. A victim may feel many different things about the crime and his or her part in it. Anger, embarrassment, disbelief, helplessness, and guilt are all common emotions experienced by crime victims. It's important to remember that although you may feel a lot of confusing things, it is possible to return to your old self. It just takes some time and work.

Being a Victim

The most frustrating experience for many victims is their search for a cause, a reason for the crime. Before becoming a victim, the world seems orderly. Things make sense. But the shock of being a victim may turn an orderly world upside down for the victim and his or her family.

Trying to fit back into his or her old life is often difficult for a victim. Following are some common reactions of victims as they try to cope:

It didn't happen to me. This is called denial.
Victims may find it too painful to accept that they
were the victim of a violent crime and will ignore
their feelings or avoid discussing the subject with
other people. They often stay very busy or sleep more
than usual to avoid thinking about the crime.

Overwhelming emotion. Some victims react with ex-
treme nervousness, depression, or anger. Some people
may stay inside all day. Others may be irritable and
anxious around their friends and may get angry with
little reason.

Anger. Some victims react by being self-destructive.
They may turn to drugs, alcohol, or dangerous behavior.
Often, they blame themselves and think of things they
may have done to cause or deserve the crime. Self-
destructive victims may refuse help from friends and
family. Some victims may even try to kill themselves.

Coping with police, family, and friends can be difficult. They may push the victim into talking about the
crime too soon. Or they may give too much space,
making the victim feel like no one cares.

These same people might talk about violence in ways
that may seem confusing or painful for a victim of violent crime. People often talk of hurting someone for
reasons that may or may not seem important to the
victim. This can make the victim question what he or
she did to deserve their pain.

More and more people are speaking out against weapons
and violent crime.

Expressing yourself. Other victims try to talk about their experience as much as possible. They find friends, family, or trained professionals to discuss their feelings about the crime. Sometimes they try to help other victims. That is often how support groups are created. Helping others can help you to accept your own feelings about being a victim.

Working it out in your head. Many victims try to learn all there is to know about what happened to them. They try to understand the crime and the way the criminal thought and felt. They use reason and logic to look for explanations for their own emotions. Many decide to see a therapist and go through the healing process together.

If you have been the victim of a violent crime, you may have gone through one or more of these reactions. Be patient with yourself. Even if it seems that no one understands your feelings, there are people who know what you are going through and who want to help. If you feel comfortable discussing the crime with family or friends, ask for their help. If you want to speak to a therapist, ask your parents, a guidance counselor, or any trusted adult for assistance in locating the right person.

Asking for Help

Lots of people think it's easy just to go up to someone and say, "I need help." But it isn't that simple. For many, asking for help is the most difficult part of being a victim. Sorting out personal

When victims of violent crime testify in court against their attacker(s), they often relive their frightening experience.

feelings may take a long time and use up all of a victim's energy. After a reasonable amount of time has passed, those close to the victim may think all is well. But he or she may still not be able to function normally.

Talking with a counselor or therapist can help a victim to work out emotional problems.

Jacob was robbed and badly beaten behind school. After the crime his mother and father were very worried about him. But Jacob seemed to handle things fine. Of course, he had been scared for a while. But his injuries healed and, all in all, his parents felt he came back to normal rather quickly. They decided Jacob was okay and didn't pay special attention to his behavior.

But in reality, Jacob felt nervous all the time. He hadn't been able to sleep well since the attack. He jumped whenever he heard a sudden noise or was approached from behind. But he didn't tell his parents, teachers or friends. Jacob felt guilty and ashamed for still being afraid. He didn't want his family or friends to think he couldn't handle himself. He stayed in his room most of the time and kept to himself at school.

Jacob's parents didn't realize that their son was still suffering mentally from his experience. Sometimes a victim feels a lot more than he or she shows on the outside. When this happens, the victim must seek help.

If you are feeling bad about being a victim, talk to someone. Never be ashamed of your feelings. If you feel a certain way, there is a good reason for it. Share your thoughts with someone you trust. And don't be afraid to let someone know you are scared. The best way to feel better about yourself after being a violent crime victim is by letting out your fear, anger, and frustration. Talking about your feelings can help you understand them, and help you get on with your life.

Ways to Get Better

Sometimes the people closest to the victim actually make him or her feel worse about the crime. Family members and friends may treat the victim as if he or she did something wrong or stupid.

- Why were you walking alone?
- Haven't we told you to be home before dark?
- Didn't you *feel* something was wrong?
- Did you attract attention to yourself?
- Didn't we warn you about that crowd?

These questions can be very hurtful. People don't want to believe that violent crime can happen to them at any time. To feel better, many people try to make the victim responsible somehow for the crime. This makes it easier for them to feel safe. In truth, you only have control over yourself. The only person to blame for the violent crime is the criminal.

Although victims are frightened and unnerved by their experience, they can find their way back to normal living. Here are some helpful positive steps victims can take after a crime.

Accept your feelings about the crime. Being the victim of a violent crime is frightening. Don't be afraid to let your anger out. There is nothing wrong with being mad, afraid, sad, or confused. These feelings become harmful only when they are kept inside, like Jacob's. Express your feelings to people you trust. It will feel good to say what's on your mind.

Emphasize the positive. It may seem that nothing good came out of your experience. But you can take what you know now and use it to help others. Start a support group where victims of violent crime can express their feelings to people who have gone through the same thing. Maybe your experience has taught you something about yourself.

Change your habits. If you can't get rid of your fear, change your schedule or your surroundings. Walk home a different way. Leave work at a different time. Wear other clothes. Do something special after school. You can put the crime behind you by putting yourself someplace new.

Reconstruct the scene. Imagine yourself in the crime situation. Confront your fears and defeat them. This time, picture yourself successfully dealing with the thing that you are frightened of the most.

Give yourself credit. You did your very best under difficult circumstances. Maybe you outwitted your attacker, or maybe you were scared and did exactly as you were told. Either way, you did okay! You survived—that's what is important.

Get the help you need. Every crime victim is different. What works for you might not work for someone else. Explore your feelings and figure out how this terrible experience has changed you and your life. Ask yourself what kind of help you would accept, and then go for it.

Today more than ever, police training tries to develop understanding
and sensitivity in officers when dealing with victims of violent crime.

Chapter 4

Your Legal Rights

For many victims of violent crime, the actual crime is only the first part of being a victim. The criminal justice system can be confusing and overwhelming. Victims often feel lost in the system. And having to tell and retell the story of the crime in front of police, judges, and lawyers can be upsetting.

After the Crime

The FBI report on crime notes that almost three out of five crimes are never reported to the police. Many people are hesitant to get involved with the criminal justice system. There are many reasons why a person might choose to keep a violent crime to him- or herself. They may be too upset or embarrassed about the crime to tell their story. They may think that the police will not believe them. Their attacker may be a family member and the victim may not want to see that person go to jail. They may fear revenge by friends of the attacker. But by choosing to remain silent, the victim will probably never see their attacker brought to justice.

Many people feel the police are insensitive to the needs of the victim of a crime. The detectives may ask questions that make the victim feel very uncomfortable. In truth, the police are not trying to make the victim upset. They are trying to find out exactly what happened so that they can find the attacker. The police need to maintain an emotional distance from the crimes they investigate. This distance may seem cold and impersonal to a victim. Because of this, police departments around the country are recognizing the need for training in how to treat victims who are still troubled by their experiences. Many detectives have learned to show respect and compassion for a victim. This sensitivity training will result in more understanding between victims and police.

Many victims feel that they are being treated as the criminal. Insensitive police can cause this reaction. But the nature of the criminal justice system is responsible and the police are required to be as professional as possible, not taking sides with the victim or the criminal. They need to fully investigate a situation to reveal the truth. They are doing their jobs and upholding the American belief that a person is innocent until proven guilty. Even if you know who your attacker is, he or she is still guaranteed a fair trial.

Citizens' groups can be effective in helping to keep their communities more crime-free.

During the investigation or trial, the victim may feel that the police should do more to protect the public and put the criminal behind bars. But the legal system acts cautiously to ensure that only the guilty person is punished for the crime. If it seems like the police are going easy on a suspected attacker, it is because as an American citizen that person is guaranteed the full attention of the law. The police do everything possible to avoid sending an innocent person to jail.

Inside the System

The best result a victim of violent crime can hope for is the opportunity to put his or her attacker in jail. Victims generally feel helpless and controlled by their attackers. Often, "getting even" through the criminal justice system can be good for the victim's recovery. Identifying and seeing that the violent offender is punished may resolve the violent crime for the victim. It may relieve the victim's feelings of helplessness and fear.

After a crime has been reported, the police come to investigate. Every victim and witness is questioned. As a victim, you will be asked to tell your story many times over the course of the investigation. The police will ask you to make a formal statement. This is your version of the crime.

During questioning it is important that you always tell the truth. Sometimes, embarrassing information comes out. Parents may find out you weren't where you told them you would be. Maybe you were doing something you shouldn't. Even if this is the case, tell the police all the facts and worry about other things later. The more information you give the police, the better the chance of arresting your attacker.

After making a statement, you may be asked to look at pictures of convicted criminals—mug shots— to identify your attacker. Take your time. Spotting your attacker in the mug books may solve the crime for the police.

If the police do find the criminal, you may be asked to identify him or her in person. This can be a very emotional experience for victims. Fear, resentment, and anger may return just from seeing the attacker again. It is important that you stay calm and be honest.

When Rosa was told the police wanted her to identify the man who raped her, she became very frightened and locked herself in her room. The thought of seeing her attacker again terrified her. It brought back horrible memories.

Rosa's mother understood how scared her daughter was. She explained to Rosa that it was important for victims to help the police. She also suggested that Rosa would feel much better knowing her rapist would be punished and off the street.

After a while, Rosa came out of her room and went to the police station. She walked into a small room with a large window on one side. She watched six men line up behind the window and face her. A policeman explained that the men could not see Rosa.

When she recognized the man who had attacked her, all the terror and pain she had felt during the rape came back. Her knees buckled. Her stomach got tight. Rosa's mother squeezed her hand and whispered softly in her ear. Rosa took a deep breath and pointed to the man who had raped her.

Ask a friend or family member to come with you when you go to the police station. Take your time and be absolutely sure of yourself when identifying your attacker. Seeing the criminal again may be frightening, but it will give you some satisfaction knowing that you helped to bring the guilty person to justice and perhaps prevented the attacker from striking again.

If the police capture the criminal and find enough evidence to prosecute, you may be asked to testify in court. This generally involves telling your story to the jury and judge. A defense lawyer and a prosecutor will ask you many questions about the attack. Describe the crime just as you remember it. Make sure you feel confident and secure before you go into court. This is the final step in the victim's search for justice.

Unfortunately, the chances that your attacker(s) will ever be brought to trial and punished are not very good. Only about 1 in every 4 crimes reported results in arrest of the criminal.

The victim of a crime may be asked to appear in court and testify if the criminal is brought to trial.

Assistance and Compensation

As you have seen, a victim's experience with
violent crime goes far beyond the crime itself.
Difficulty with the police and court systems may
end up making the victim feel as powerless and
frustrated as when he or she was attacked. For the
poor, dealing with the crime after it occurs can be
even worse. The process of healing is sometimes
an expensive one.

If you have physical or psychological injuries,
getting the help you need may seem impossible
because of the high cost of doctors and counselors,
but don't get discouraged. Discuss the situation
with your parents. There are resources available to
you. (See the Where to Get Help section in this
book.) Many states have crime victim compensation laws. These provide money for medical and
legal expenses resulting from the crime. Ask the
police or the prosecutor involved with your case if
your state has a crime victim assistance program.

Most victims of violent crime expect payment
in one form or another. This may or may not happen. After a crime, family and friends may care for
the victim for a period of time, assisting through
recovery. In some ways, helping to put the criminal behind bars is compensation for the victim.
Knowing that justice has been done can be a very
powerful healer.

In rare cases, the cause of the crime can be
related to the carelessness of others. If you have

been the victim of a violent crime that was caused by someone else's negligence, you may seek compensation by suing the person or institution responsible. This procedure, a civil suit, is separate from the prosecution of the criminal. You probably will not be eligible to receive financial help for this type of legal expense. (The Legal Aid Society is a nonprofit, legal service agency that is available to all persons regardless of their ability to pay. However, Legal Aid does not handle civil suits.)

To proceed with such a lawsuit you will need to hire an attorney to represent your claim in a court of law. The legal system can be overwhelming. But don't let it frighten you out of your rights. As an American citizen you are entitled to justice. The only way to find it is through the police and the courts. The law really is on your side. Be patient.

Organized "block watch" groups usually are made up of neighbors looking out for one another.

Chapter 5

Crime Prevention

The best way to avoid being a victim of violent crime is by taking action now. You can protect yourself and your community. Something as small as the way you walk may discourage a mugger from attacking you. The only way to improve your chances is by taking an active role in the battle against violent crime.

The Battle Against Violent Crime

The United States has made terrific progress in reducing violent crime in its schools, cities, and towns. After years of rising crime rates and escalating violence, crime rates in big cities decreased for the first time in a decade in 1994. In 1995 and 1996, this decrease in the number of violent crimes continued. There was a 4 percent overall decrease in violent crime in 1995.

It is important to remember that any violent crime is too much. Even with the decreases of the last few years, the United States still has the highest crime rate among the world's major industrial countries. As far as we've come, we still have a long way to go.

Unfortunately, our society sometimes sends mixed messages about violence. Television and movies glamorize violence through heroes who use violence as a solution. Today's television shows and movies include graphic violence as a way to attract audiences. Because this violence is seen by millions of people everyday, we get used to it. Violence becomes a part of our lives and it no longer surprises us. This acceptance is dangerous.

Adults and children talk boldly about violence when they say things like "I'm going to kill the guy who scratched my car." While this may sound impressive and make one person feel important, it contributes to the feeling that violence is an acceptable part of life.

The best way to prevent violence is to inform yourself about violent crime and take steps to make yourself less likely to become a victim. You can learn to understand and appreciate the police so that they can do their job more effectively. You can join a community group that watches over a neighborhood. You can take a self-defense course and learn how to protect yourself. We need more people to step up and say no to crime before it can start. Instead of expecting others to stop the violence, you need to take action yourself.

Personal Safety

You should always put your safety ahead of your convenience. Don't worry about walking an extra couple of blocks if it means that you can avoid a dangerous neighborhood. Take the time to be aware of yourself and your surroundings. It may save you from being a victim.

J.J. Bittenbinder is a homicide detective in Chicago. He has taught many people the best ways to avoid being a victim of violent crime on the streets.

Make yourself a tougher target. Be smart on the streets. In this case, your image is everything. Walk confidently even if you are nervous. Don't walk with your eyes staring at the ground or the sky. You should always focus on things going on in front and around you.

Deny privacy. This just means staying away from anyone who seems dangerous. Avoid streets you know will be empty. Don't take shortcuts through strange areas. Don't be afraid to walk right into a store or anywhere with a lot of people if you feel nervous. Whenever you can, walk with a friend.

Attract attention if you're in trouble. Yell and scream as loud as you can. Don't feel silly. Protect yourself by waking up the whole neighborhood if you have to.

Take action. Take positive steps toward your own safety. Learn how to defend yourself. Sometimes it is impossible to avoid dealing with violent

Learning self-defense techniques promotes self-confidence.

crime. When you have to do something to protect yourself, do it with all your energy and attention. The only way to defend yourself well is by being confident in your actions.

Be aware of your appearance. Don't have lots of expensive things visible on your body. If you just got a new watch, don't run up to everyone you see and show it off.

Tanya wears nice clothes and enjoys looking good. But she's smart about being too noticeable. For her last birthday her father gave her a gold bracelet. Even though she would like to wear it to school, she knows it wouldn't be safe. She saves it for special occasions.

Keep to yourself. The old saying about not talking to strangers is still true. You don't have to answer if someone speaks to you. If it's a conversation you don't want to have, then keep walking. It's good to help when people are in need, but on the streets you must be concerned with your own safety first. When you are safe, then you think about helping.

One day on her way to school, a car pulled up beside Jessica. The man inside started to talk to her, but Jessica just ignored him. She felt that something was wrong, so she didn't bother answering him. She went into the first open store she saw and remained there until he drove away.

Be aware of your neighborhood. If it's not safe, do something about it. Don't be afraid to tell people about a suspicious incident or strangers that seem to be hanging around.

Joe noticed that three streetlights had burned out on his block. A large middle section of his street was dark. Just looking at it made him a little nervous. The next morning he reported it to the town maintenance department. Two days later, the lights were repaired. The street seemed much safer.

Know where you're going. If you're visiting someone's house, make sure you know where it is before you start. Try to get specific details, like house color, style, or a description of something that is nearby. A person who looks lost is an easy target for crime.

Whenever Ben rides the bus, he checks his map first. He makes sure he knows what bus to take and where to get off. Sometimes he writes the directions down, so he can glance at them if he needs to.

Personal safety may require a total change in your behavior. You have to be safety-conscious every day and force yourself to do the little things. Being street-smart has to become a habit. You won't always have time to think about it. By knowing the facts about personal safety, you are joining the battle against violent crime.

It is safer to walk with friends than to walk alone, especially at night.

School Safety

Although violence in schools is down in the last few years in the United States, schools are less safe than they were fifteen years ago. Drugs, gangs, and weapons have turned schools into places of fear for many students.

The police and politicians take these problems very seriously. In 1996, the Anti-Gang and Youth Violence Control Act was passed by Congress to encourage teens to avoid violence. This new set of laws put aside money to buy computers to monitor gang activity and to build jails for teens repeatedly convicted of violent crime. These laws on their own cannot stop violence in schools. What they can do is remove some of those students who have already committed violent crimes and who are most likely to commit these crimes again. Students and teachers can then work together to build understanding and hopefully stop the violence.

There are some simple rules you can follow to make yourself a less likely target in your school:

Be aware of the "high-risk" areas. Bathrooms, locker rooms, cafeterias, and gyms are all common locations for violent crime in school. You can't always avoid these places, but be aware when you find yourself in one of them. Stick with at least one other person when in these areas, especially after normal school hours.

Get involved. Join a club or two. Participate in school activities. Run for student government positions. The more people you know, the safer you will be. Learn other student's first names, and make sure they know yours. Loners are always the easiest victims.

Don't be intimidated. If something concerns you, let somebody know. Don't be afraid to talk to your parents or a teacher about your fears. If you are worried about someone getting even, talk about that, too. You don't have to name names if you don't want to.

Many schools have programs that teach kids how to handle crime. By teaching awareness and safety, schools have involved their students in the fight against violent crime. One such program, sponsored by the FBI, is called TIPS (Teaching Individual Protective Strategies). TIPS brings students together for discussions, exercises, and games designed to increase safety and awareness. Students learn to have respect for others' opinions, to settle disagreements without violence, and to take simple steps toward everyday crime prevention. Students learn about crime from the experts and from one another.

Find out if your school has a program like TIPS. If not, talk to friends and teachers about starting one.

Crime Prevention in Your Community

The only way to fight crime effectively is by involving everyone. This is why community-based prevention is so important. It's easier to make a difference when you know that your neighbors and friends are behind you.

Fernando Mateo, left, originator of the program to exchange merchandise for guns, inspects surrendered weapons. New York City Police Commissioner Raymond Kelly is with him.

Police departments are recognizing the need to develop good relations with communities. In the last few years, police officers in cities such as New York have worked hard to develop new ties with ordinary citizens. The police track all of the crimes in the city with a computer to see where crime is on the rise. Then they send as many officers as necessary to those neighborhoods to show criminals that the police won't let crime happen there.

This hard work has paid off. People feel more comfortable telling the police about crimes they have witnessed. The police show more respect for ordinary people. Criminals can't hang out without being noticed anymore. In New York and many other cities, crime is down.

The key is to get involved. Your area may have a neighborhood watch group, sometimes called a block watch. In these groups, members of the community make crime prevention a personal responsibility. Sometimes regular citizens patrol the streets at night. If they see suspicious activity, they notify the police.

If your neighborhood doesn't already have one of these groups, speak to your parents about starting one. You can also fight crime in your community just by keeping your eyes open. Pay attention to what is normal activity and what is different. Get to know your neighbors. Report to your parents anything or anyone that seems suspicious. Share what you know about safety. Take a stand in the fight against violent crime.

Glossary—*Explaining New Words*

adrenaline A hormone secreted by the adrenal glands that increases endurance and muscular strength.

assault An unlawful threat or attempt to physically harm someone; a violent attack.

compensation Money or services given to some victims to make up for the crime and assist in recovery.

criminal Someone who commits a crime.

criminal justice system The police and courts; a way of finding the guilty person and punishing him or her for the crime.

defense lawyer Person in charge of helping the accused person get a fair trial.

denial Refusing to accept that the crime happened to you.

homicide An act in which one person causes the death of another.

jury A group of ordinary people sworn to hear evidence in a law case and give a decision about the guilt or innocence of the accused person.

prosecutor Lawyer in charge of proving that the accused person is guilty of the crime.

psychological Affecting the mind; mental.

rape Forcing someone to have sexual intercourse.

robbery Stealing from someone with a threat or attempt of violence.

sensitivity training Special sessions that help people to gain a deeper understanding of themselves and others.

support group People who have similar problems who get together to help each other by talking about their feelings and experiences.

testify To declare publicly, especially under oath in court.

therapist Someone who is trained to help victims express and accept their feelings about the crime.

victim Someone who is threatened or attacked.

vulnerable Easily hurt.

witness Someone who sees a crime happen.

Where to Go for Help

In the U.S.
Coalition to Stop Gun Violence
100 Maryland Avenue, NE
Washington, DC 20001-5625
(202) 530-0340
Web site: http://www.gun free.org

National Council on Alcohol and Drug Dependence
    (NCADD)
12 W. 21st Street
New York, NY 10010
(800) 622-2255
fax (212) 645-1690
Web site: http://www.ncadd.org/
e-mail: national@NCADD.org

National Crime Prevention Council
1700 K Street, NW Second Floor
Washington, DC 20006
(202) 466-NCPC
Web site: http://www.we prevent.org

National Organization for Victim Assistance
1757 Park Road, NW
Washington, DC 20010
(800) 879-6682

National School Safety Center
4165 Thousand Oaks Boulevard, Suite 290
Westlake Village, CA 91362
(805) 373-9977
Web site: http://www. msscl.org
e-mail: june@msscl.org

Prepare Self-Defense
25 West 43rd Street
New York, NY 10036
(800) 442-7273

The Washington D.C. Rape Crisis Center Hot Line
    (for a nationwide listing of rape crisis centers)
(202) 333-7273

In Canada
Canadians Concerned About Violence in
    Entertainment (C-CAVE)
167 Glen Road
Toronto, ON M4W 2W8
(416) 961-1853

Toronto Rape Crisis Centre Hot Line
(416) 597-8808

Victims of Violence National Inc.
Unit 2, 220 Mulock Drive
Newmarket, ON L3Y 7V1
(416) 836-1010

1-800-VICTIMS

For Further Reading

Cole, George F. *The American System of Criminal Justice.* Belmont, CA: Brooks/Cole, 1989.

Krista, Alix. *Victims: Surviving the Aftermath of Violent Crime.* London: Century, 1990.

Miller, Maryann. *Coping with Weapons and Violence in School and on Your Streets.* New York: The Rosen Publishing Group, 1993.

Schleifer, Jay. *Everything You Need to Know About Weapons in School and at Home.* New York: The Rosen Publishing Group, 1994.

Toch, Thomas, and Marc Silver. "Violence in Schools." *U.S. News and World Report*, November 8, 1993, p. 30.

Index

About the Author
Jed Palmer is a freelance writer. He has lived in New York all his life, and currently works at a publishing company in Manhattan.

Photo Credits
Cover photo by Stuart Rabinowitz; photos on pp. 2, 11, 19, 32, 43, 53 by Norma Mondazzi; pp. 8, 14, 31, 36, 39, 50, 56 © AP/ Wide World Photos; p. 21 by Kim Sonsky, p. 24 © Paul Howell/Gamma Liaison; p. 29 © David Woo/Gamma Liaison; p. 46 by Blackbirch Graphics, Inc.